GROW YOUR WEALTH

Smart ways to grow money twice as fast

****

HELENA WRIGHT

Legal & Disclaimer

The information contained in this book is not designed to replace or take the place of any form of medicine or professional medical advice. The information in this book has been provided for educational and entertainment purposes only.

The information contained in this book has been compiled from sources deemed reliable, and it is accurate to the best of the Author's knowledge; however, the Author cannot guarantee its accuracy and validity and cannot be held liable for any errors or omissions. Changes are periodically made to this book. You must consult your doctor or get professional medical advice before using any of the suggested remedies, techniques, or information in this book.

Upon using the information contained in this book, you agree to hold harmless the Author from and against any damages, costs, and expenses, including any legal fees potentially resulting from the application of any of the information provided by this guide. This disclaimer applies to any damages or injury caused by the use and application, whether directly or indirectly, of any advice or information presented, whether for breach of contract, tort, negligence, personal injury, criminal intent, or under any other cause of action.

You agree to accept all risks of using the information presented inside this book. You need to consult a professional medical practitioner in order to ensure you are both able and healthy enough to participate in this program.

Table of Contents

Introduction

Becoming wealthy is not a passive activity that one can engage in here and there, putting in minimal effort. If you want to become wealthy, know this: each and every step you take in climbing the proverbial ladder towards wealth will be difficult. It is not going to be easy. Let this sink in. Becoming wealthy and maintaining that wealth—abiding by the habits of the rich—is going to be hard work. It will be grueling. It will be time consuming. It will change your habits, your routines and it will change your life as a whole. Take into account that your riches will not occur overnight. Wealth is long-term. There are no secrets and no "get rich quick" schemes to acquiring wealth. You have to make smart choices, save, invest, and again you have to be willing to put in the work. Work. Work. Work. You have to believe in yourself and back up that belief with action. These are things you have to realize and commit yourself to before moving on. Are you ready to make these changes and begin building your wealth?

Prioritize your energy. Think actively. Use your time wisely. Focus. Don't allow yourself to become distracted when it comes to your wealth. This is your livelihood, your well-being and peace of mind. Invest your accrued money in ways that will help it grow. Do your research. Remember: long-term. Remember: this is not going to be a short process. Remember: "get rich quick" schemes should not corrupt your thoughts. "Get rich quick" steals your energy, takes away your time and leaves you worse off than you were before. "Get rich quick" schemes are the passive way to acquiring riches. And what is the passive way to acquire wealth? There is no passive way. You have to stay active with your energy, your time and your money. You must always keep focus on your larger, long-term vision of wealth.

You are not on a game show walking away with thousands in one evening. You are not a character in a fairy tale. You will get jerked around, knocked down, but the thing that defines the rich—meaning those that have built their wealth on their own—is that they *always* get back up. They always believe in their goals and will let nothing stop them. This is the attitude that they have and that you must work towards acquiring. You must visualize and realize where you want to be. But that alone is not enough. You need to put in the hours, the energy, the time, and yes, the money in order to see your equity grow. You need to put your blood, sweat and tears into this.

4

Laziness is not a word that you will include in your personal dictionary any more.

Ask yourself; why do you want to become wealthy? How are you going to do it? You will find guidelines and answers here, but remember that your vision, your perseverance and your persistence in the long-term will define whether or not you will succeed.

Chapter 1

How to start?

Define Your Long-Term Goals

Whether you are 25 or 55, there is always time to achieve your goals. There is always time for you to set goals. Goals are imperative to the process of becoming wealthy. They give you something to work for and look forward to. Goals are the habits of the rich and wealthy. Be active and focused on our goals, set them realistically and work, keep active, towards reaching them. If you are thinking that you don't need to put in the work, that you will make money and you don't have to try in order to reach a certain amount, then you aren't ready to make the plunge. You aren't ready to grow your money and live like the wealthy do. Your routine and your habits should be based around your goals and how you are going to achieve them.

If you want to become wealthy, you need to set long-term goals that adhere to the amount of money you are hoping to make. You should have a number of goals. How much money do you want to have in 5 years? Are you saving for a house? Saving for a car? Saving for your children's college education?

How important is each goal? You're going to want to rate each one for importance. For the more important goals you want to prioritize your funds to meet them first. Ideally, you're going to want to achieve all of your goals. But let yourself be realistic. What goals must you keep? Keep yourself active. You are never passive in regards to your goals.

Take action now! A bonus free gift "Wealth-Tool" for you to guide you in your reading. Grab a copy at http://livingthelifeuwant.com/wealth-tool/, & start benefiting from it.

Do not expect it to be easy. Set your goals high. You never want to make it easy on yourself in regards to achieving your long-term financial milestones. It might seem impossible—that is good. If you want to become wealthy, you will figure out ways to make payments to your savings and investments. This will grow and solidify good traits in your character. You are learning and acquiring the traits of the rich. It will not happen overnight. It will take years. That is why you are going after long-term goals.

Think it terms of years. Not weeks or months. Setting your goals at five year increments is a good way to start.

Stick to a budget. Figure out how much you are spending and what you are spending it on. You will most likely be surprised at how much of your equity is spent on things you don't need. You will realize that you can cut out these extra, cash-leeching extras. Learn to budget yourself. Find out where you can spend less. Becoming wealthy has much to do with being frugal.

Unfortunately, you can't always trust your best intentions. Say you intend to put away a certain amount of money each week. You start off strong and then as time goes on, you start to tell yourself, "I'll put a little less in this week and next week I'll put more money in." And then begins the downward spiral. You justify your excess spending. You put less and less into your savings and investments. You tell yourself you don't need to save so much anyway. You change your goals and you fall off from your original plan.

For this reason, you need to train yourself. You need to teach yourself that, no matter what, you are going to stick to your goals. Sticking to your goals is a habit of the wealthy. You want to become wealthy. In order to stick to those goals, in order to avoid falling off the train, you're going to want to set up automatic payments. These payments will be deducted from your check every time you are paid. The money will be transferred straight from your pay into your investments. This way, you aren't going to be able to spend the money that you no longer have. It will be out of your hands and your willpower will not be tested. This will teach you to follow your budget. You need to have structured before you are strong enough to stand on your own. Which brings me to my next point; get rid of your credit cards and just stick to your debit, otherwise you will be tempted to spend money you don't have and it will be easy to fall into debt.

Be wary of your emotions. The market will go up. The market will go down. This is inevitable. This is called volatility. Essentially it is the range in which the market moves up and down. You should know now that everyone's investments go through rough patches. There are ways to minimize loss and risk, but there is no way to be 100% protected against losing money. Stick to your guns during the hard times. You've set up your goals for a reason and you don't want to withdraw your money at the first sign of a rough patch. Be cautious, but also be smart.

Plan your goals to be as low-risk as possible. As stated before, be careful of your emotions. You might want to jump on a hot stock or be quick to sell when one is plummeting. Just hang on. Be patient. Realize again that the market is volatile and it is best to stick to the goals you have set up for yourself. Never rush into anything. Get advice. Sleep on it. Always be thinking about your goals.

You cannot be passive when reaching for wealth. You must always remain active and be ready to rebalance your assets if needed. Be patient. Don't rush. These things have been stated before. But, and there's a big but, you must always be monitoring how your investments are doing. Keep them balanced and beware of any high-risk investments. "Get rich quick"—always avoid this. Even if you're told that it is a sure thing. Always be sceptical of fast ways to make money. You want to focus on the long-term. This is how the wealthy operate. They have the patience and the smarts to stick to a well thought-out, prepared and balanced plan. They stick to their goals. And they get knocked off the boat. They get pushed to the ground. But they always stick to their vision of what the future will be. Stay focused. Stay active and be persistent. Be resilient. Do not get lazy when it comes to your money. Always be on the ball and over time, you will reach your goals. You will increase your wealth as long as you are giving your all.

Chapter 2

What you should do.

Set up Savings Plan & Stick to It

To wish to be wealthy is not enough. To envision yourself as wealthy is not enough. Even to believe in yourself, which is very important, is not enough. Setting up a budget is essential. It keeps you active in your journey to wealth. It is integral in your journey to wealth. It enables you, at all times, to be aware of what money you have. It enables you to be aware of where your money is going. It will help you to cut out unneeded expenses. It will enable you to realize where you can save money and gives you a framework of your equity.

If you want to adopt the habits of the rich, you must have a budget. If you think you can get by without a budget, you are being passive. You are letting laziness get the better of you. Maybe you are afraid about what a budget will reveal. Even more reason to start one. It is central to your hopes for growing wealth. It enables you to be in complete control of your monetary destiny. You are only able to grow what you know you have.

People waste money every day. Something little here and something little there. Little things added to little things added to little things. Every day. When these little things add up, they become one thing. One big thing. And this big thing is what you are going to need to cut out in order to make a rise. In order to increase your wealth and get into the levels of real wealth, you are going to need to be aware of where every facet of your money is going. Do not leave it up to fate. From now on, you are your own fate.

So, it's time for you to start making that budget. And you are not only making a budget, but you are also going to tell yourself that you need to stick to the budget you create. If you want to grow your equity and start adopting the rituals and habits of those who have already made it, then you need to make sure to stick with it. You have to adopt the budget and stay consistent with it. If you want to stray, remember your goals.

It's time for you to figure out exactly what you are making. If you get paid weekly or bi-weekly or even monthly, it doesn't matter. You need to figure out how much money you are pulling in each time you get paid. Figure out what you are making after taxes. If money is taken out for insurance, figure out how much you are making after that. Figure out how much of that money is able to make it to your bank account and then go from there. Then figure out how much of your money is coming in each month. Planning your budget monthly is a good way to get started—most of your bills are paid monthly. Thus, it is a good rule of thumb to calculate at the monthly level.

Next, it's time to calculate your expenses. Now, this is split up into a few steps. Take a breath, there is no need or time for you to get overwhelmed. You want to take control of your monetary fate. It's time to calculate into your budget the expenses you have each month that do not fluctuate. You should be calculating into your budget expenses such as student loans, your mortgage or rent, your car insurance payments, etc. You want to discern what expenses you have that are going to be consistent each month.

If you have not downloaded the bonus free gift "Wealth-Tool", grab a copy now at http://livingthelifeuwant.com/wealth-tool/, & you will be guided step-by-step as you read along. Benefit it. It's free anyway.

A side tip: always make a list of what you need before you go out to shop. Always stick to the list and over time, you will find ways to cut a few dollars here and there. In the long run, those dollars here and there add up to serious money. If you do this every time you go out shopping—whether it be for groceries, clothes, household necessities—you will eventually be cutting back on spending every time you go out. And this, like mentioned before, adds up. A few dollars here and a few dollars there, in the long run, turns out to be much more than a few dollars. You are always in control of what you are spending, even if you don't want to believe it. Do not be passive in any aspect of your money. Always be active and be focused enough to realize when dollars are needlessly slipping away. If you think it's too hard, then you don't want to be wealthy. The rich made it to where they are by cutting out their extraneous costs any time they were able.

It's now time to figure out what expenses you have that do fluctuate. Think about expenses that vary each month. Your grocery bill, monthly. Each of your utility bills. Think about your cell phone bill. Think about what you are spending on your television bill. Your internet bill. Take into account what you spend on entertainment—going out for a drink, going out to a restaurant, the movies, going to sports games, concerts, etc. These are expenses that change from month to month. These expenses are the ones you have control over. It is essential that you find ways, even subtle ones, to cut these varying expenses. And if you want to live as the wealthy do, no matter how hard it is you are going to find ways to cut back in this department each month.

And how are you going to cut back on these fluctuating expenses? You are going to rank individually each changing expense that you have. What is most important on this list? What is the least important? And from this point, you will be able to see clearly where you are able to make some changes. Remember: this is for your future and your goals. Remember: do not let this overwhelm you. You want to have control over your money because, otherwise, why are you going to work all the time? Making a budget means that you can get beyond making ends meet. It means you can begin to get ahead and find out how.

Lastly, and to hammer the point home, you want to know where every dollar is going. It doesn't matter if you are using a cell phone app, a computer program like excel, or pencil and notebook, you want to write down every expense you have, every day, for the month. Remember: every nickel and dime over ten years becomes more than just nickels and dimes. It's a lot of nickels and dimes. So for this reason, every time money leaves your possession, you want to have record of how much and what the money was spent on. In this way, you are able to see what areas of your spending are extraneous. And once you find out where you are spending needlessly, you are able to cut that needless spending out of your life.

Chapter 3
Track it.

Money Management is a Job

As you can understand with creating a budget, keeping track of where your money is not easy. For that reason, money management is a job. You must treat it like a job. Money management is crucial and without an overseeing set of eyes, your money will not grow. No matter how much you are making, if you are not keeping track of where you money is going and what it is doing, you will not grasp what it is to be and remain wealthy. Those who are wealthy and remain wealthy are only where they are because they have managed their money well. They haven't been passive in regards to where their cash is flowing. They are actively monitoring their savings, their investments, their income and their expenses. Money management is a job. But don't think that you aren't getting paid for it. Even though you may not be receiving a pay check for your efforts, you can find solace in the fact that you are in control of your money's fate. You will know where money is slipping through the cracks and how to stop it. You will find that managing your wealth is as important as making an income.

Keeping track of your budget is part of money management, but it is not the whole of it. Along the same page of keeping a budget, but still different, is figuring your net worth. You want to be in control of your money and therefore it is central to your money management that you are aware of your net worth.

What is net worth? Basically it is everything that you own—savings, stocks, bonds, vehicles, houses, land, valuables, musical instruments, artwork etc. Add up the value of all your belongings. Then figure out what sort of debts you owe—credit cards, car payments, insurance, utilities, and so on. If you're keeping your budget right, you should have a good idea of the debts that you owe. In simple terms, net worth is your big-picture budget. What is all the money you have available to you right at this moment? You should know what the wealthy would ask after figuring their net worth: How can I increase it?

This is where everything is coming together. Your goals will play into your net worth. Your goals will focus on increasing your net worth. Make sure to think about the long-term.

Hope you are making use of the bonus free gift "Wealth-Tool" to have clarity on your goals & savings plan to increase your net worth twice as fast. Grab a copy now at http://livingthelifeuwant.com/wealth-tool/ if you have not done so, & start benefiting from it.

Determine whether it may be in your best interest to rent or lease rather than buy. Automobiles will decrease in value the instance that you cruise out of the dealership. In this case, it may be better for you to lease and reap the benefits that come from that. In this way you can protect against the devaluing of the car.

It is no secret that the wealthy have exceptional credit. Credit cards are a double-edged sword: used in the wrong manner and they will severely hurt your financial credibility—your credit. Used in the right manner—and remember, you want to establish the habits of the wealthy—your credit cards will become very important tools as manager of your money.

Good credit will afford you better interest rates if applying for a loan. This can be extremely important if you find yourself applying for a mortgage or loan to start a business. Your lower interest rates, over the long run—and remember, you should always be looking at the big picture when it comes to your wealth—will save you more than just nickels and dimes. In most cases, you'll find yourself saving thousands and maybe even tens of thousands because of your lower interest rates. And your lower interest rates come about from your high credit rating.

Auto insurance is an expense that, in your budget, does not fluctuate. But there is a catch here: you can achieve lower car insurance rates initially if your credit is good. Again: nickels and dimes. But, as you know, with car insurance nickels and dimes are actually dollars and hundreds of dollars.

And in the long run—the big picture you should always be imagining—those dollars and hundreds of dollars with accrue into thousands. You, like the wealthy, need to be actively considering the ways in which you can stretch your wallet—good credit is a way to achieve that.

Beware of fees for rewards cards, but in most cases these lines of credit will benefit you. Prizes, cash back and free airfare are all things you can find yourself attaining with good credit. And, of course, make sure you are always on time with your payments and that you are paying off your debts in full—interest can be a killer.

Here is a good rule of thumb to follow when it comes to credit cards: add up your total available credit. To do this, add up the maximum credit limits for all your cards. Then add up your debts on all of your cards. The rule of thumb is this: make sure that you are using less than 30% of your available credit. Your credit score will thank you for doing so.

Make sure that you have an emergency fund established. Your car breaks down. Your hot water heater is on its last breath. The air conditioner needs to be replaced. A pipe bursts in your basement. There are myriad emergencies that can occur at any given time and there is no way to avoid this risk in life. What you can do is prepare yourself in case something like this happens.

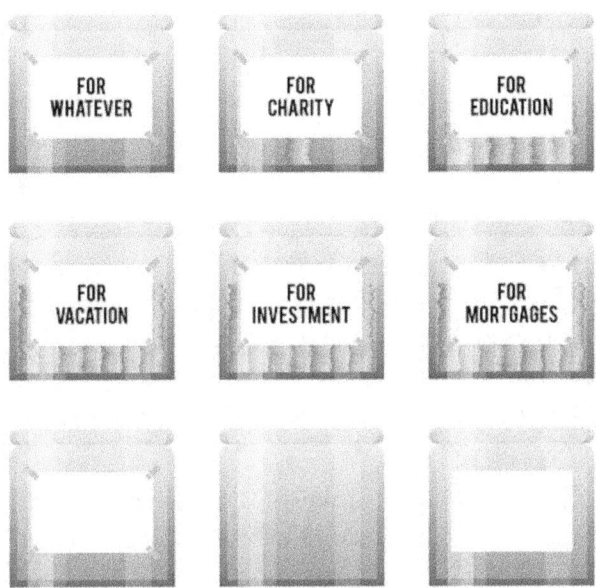

In an emergency, you want to make sure that you are not spending money that you don't have. This is one of the most important lessons to remember—the wealthy certainly know and live by it. Just to place emphasis on this point: do not spend money that you don't have!

Do not take the chance of not having insurance. Getting to the emergency room in an ambulance alone can cost thousands. Never take this chance. Life insurance. It is not pleasant to think about, of course, but if you want to become wealthy and acquire the habits of those who have money, this is something you have to do. In the sad case of a spouse perishing, you need to be prepared. As someone striving towards wealth, you must always be prepared. Homeowner's insurance. If anything unexpected happens to your home, your insurance will cover it. If you shrug it off, you might find yourself in the hole for thousands, tens of thousands, even hundreds of thousands.

Remember: reduce your risk.

Remember: do not gamble with your equity.

Remember: "better safe than sorry."

Chapter 4

Think Creatively...

Have an open mind. Be resourceful & proactive.

Realize that money is not something that hides from you, runs away, and is never attainable. In fact, you must know and realize that it *is attainable*. And not only is it attainable, realize—really dig deep now—and tell yourself that "I can be rich, I will be rich, I will do everything I can to be what I want." Garner yourself a vision: create an image of success in your head.

Set your goals. Set up a budget. Invest. But also, importantly, get creative. There are ways for you to make money by getting out of that box everyone is in.

The wealthy make it a habit to not get too comfortable. Why shouldn't you get comfortable? Because always adhering to your comfort zone will extinguish opportunities to increase your net worth. If you are not willing or ready to change—if you are shutting the shades to new horizons—then you may as well be a passive spectator to your money. If you are active, you are always exploring new routes. New and creative ways to make money and increase your net worth are everywhere these days. The age we are in is one of technology, and if you are thinking out of that so called box, then there are opportunities abounding.

IDEA + **WORK** = **SUCCESS**

Are you good at finding deals? Try your hand at a little website called Ebay. All jokes aside, if you enjoy searching around for sales and steals (you should always be, if you are trying to be wealthy-minded) then you should not have much trouble here. Buying cheap and selling for a profit with the help of this famous online market can provide you with another stream of revenue. Allotting a few hours a week to Ebay, over the long run, can net you some good money. This good money can be put towards investments. And that invested money can earn you more money and so on.

Free stuff and flexible hours. These things can be yours if you tack on a few hours of work a week as a mystery shopper. Go into a store, pretend to be a shopper. Rate the store. Buy something and be reimbursed for it. Add another stream of revenue into your equity. Get creative—if you are doing this and the Ebay route, no one said you can't sell your reimbursed, free items. The deeper you dig, the more you will realize connections and the potential for more financial growth.

Enjoy offering your opinions? Then remember this: market research. Keep your eyes open for opportunities to be part of a focus group. It's usually simple, generally only takes a few hours and often times pays well. Throw a few of these checks into your revenue every month and over five or ten years this short, part-time gig will net you some decent cash. Remember: think long-term. Every little bit counts and the more little bits that you can accrue will eventually become big bits.

Do you have an extra room in your home or apartment? Consider subletting and have an extra revenue stream that, in essence, doesn't require you to do much at all. For renting your room out long-term, give Craigslist a shot. Or maybe you don't want a full-time roommate? Airbnb.com is a great way for you to make some cash by renting out your extra room short-term. Remember: get out of your comfort zone. You could end up meeting someone with good connections in this way. Or maybe you end up meeting a good friend. Either way, subletting is a good way to bring in money without breaking a sweat.

Say you just moved to the city and your car isn't being used. Maybe you have an extra car that is sitting and costing you extra money. Check out Getaround.com. Sign up and rent out that dust-collecting, money draining extra car for yet another revenue stream. An added bonus: there are no fees and insurance is included for all rentals.

Recycling. You should be doing it anyway, but why not make a couple of extra bucks doing it? There's plenty of recycle centers out there that will give you money for your discarded aluminium. You aren't going to be able to buy a vacation home with the profits, but again, over time any type of constant revenue will turn from nickels and dimes into hundreds, even thousands of dollars.

Be a part-time taxi driver. Uber, a company that pays you to use your car to give rides, is now a $50 billion dollar company. Especially if you are near a city, this is a good way to stash away some extra money. There is also their competitor, Lyft. Sign up as a driver for one of these companies and give people rides when you have some free time. Especially if you are free during rush hour or weekend nights, you can pump some decent cash into your net worth.

A few other things to consider: house-sitting, coaching, being a personal shopper for someone that is disabled, pet-sitting, being someone's virtual assistant through Zirtual.com. Are you a fast typist? Try online transcription services and get paid by the word. Start a podcast and make money through advertisements. Have a website? Sell the advertising space. With the internet and your gung-ho attitude, the possibilities to create multiple and additional revenue streams are vast.

Make use of the bonus free gift "Wealth-Tool" to help you work out your plan. Grab a copy at http://livingthelifeuwant.com/wealth-tool/, & start benefiting from it.

Chapter 5

Diversify *Your Financial Portfolio*

Spread your risk & work for high investment returns

You know the phrase, as cliché as it is, "Don't put all your eggs into one basket." So what does that mean for investing your hard earned cash? A lot. But of course, we aren't talking about eggs and we aren't talking about baskets. We are talking about stocks and investments.

To grow your wealth, it is imperative that you do not throw your savings into one stock. No one that invests their money into the stock market needs to be a genius. You can play it safe. It doesn't need to be a gamble. While it isn't exactly the same, you wouldn't cash in your savings at the roulette table and throw it all on black. Although there are better odds than on the roulette table for you to increase your wealth through trusted, secure corporations you still do not want to "put all your eggs in one basket."

Subtract from your risk. Remember: think long-term. Your goals are not for a huge, instant gain—this, again, is the "get rich quick," passive approach. And as mentioned before, it is not in your best interest to invest in one stock alone. So, what do you think would be a good idea here? Invest your equity in different, trusted and secure corporations—spread out your money like seeds over fertile land and see it grow. That fertile land being the stock market.

Do not just invest in the computer industry. Do not just invest in the energy industry. Do not just invest in the clothing industry. You should be seeing it now or getting closer to understanding the point here. You do not want to gamble. You want your money to increase and for this reason you need to be there at every stage of your equity's growth. Your equity is your wealth, your well-being. You want to see that well-being grow. You need to stay active and monitor it at every stage of its growth. Just like the seedlings on the farm, your wealth, spread out on this fertile land of the stock market needs to be monitored actively. Be focused.

Do not just invest in the aviation industry. Do not just invest in the agriculture industry. The point is here is that you will stymie the gamble of your wealth by diversifying your stocks further. Further than just spreading equity out over many stocks. You want to extinguish risk further by investing in different trusted, secure companies throughout many industries. Say the aviation industry is going through rough times—and remember that with stocks, the bad times do occur—then again "do not have all your eggs in one basket" and for that matter, even one industry. So when this occurs, your stocks in the other industries continue to grow and your wealth, your equity, is able to endure and continue.

Be cautious about mutual funds. Mutual funds enable you to diversify your finances, but it often in one industry. Do not just invest in the healthcare industry. See what is going on here. You are still achieving diversification, but it is only on one level. That level usually being one industry. So for this reason, watch out for mutual funds.

Look into balanced funds. These are investments in which your wealth, generally, is spread out amongst different industries in the stock market. Your wealth is also spread out over bonds. In most cases, bonds will pay you money with a fixed interest rate. This payment of interest on the bond, again in most cases, pays you twice a year until the bond matures. When the bond matures, you receive the money that you originally put out for the bond.

Balanced funds also put your cash in money market accounts. Money market accounts are generally short-term investments that increase your wealth with interest. Money that you pour into the money market account gathers interest. Money market investments usually pay off over the short-term—generally under a year.

Balanced funds are a good way of skimming the risk from your investments. Balanced funds are a good way to increase wealth over time. This is always the game with investments. Time. Wait. Be patient.

However you wish to set up your portfolio, make sure it is diversified. Monitor your investments once a year at least. Keep an eye on what is going on. Remember: you need to be present. You need to be aware and 100% active in what is going on with your stocks. If you want to live like the wealthy, you don't want to leave all the work to the professionals. You want to have a grasp on what is going on with your money. You want to have a good base of knowledge to rely upon and you constantly should be learning more about the upkeep of your portfolio. Keep learning. Go beyond the advice being offered here. There is no passivity in gaining and maintaining your wealth. Remember that.

A good rule of thumb, if you choose to take the recommended conservative route, is to have about half your money invested in bonds. Bonds are generally the safest investments. Although, you must remember, with any investment there is going to be risk. This is unavoidable, but you can protect yourself the most if you can be patient and take a conservative approach to growing your money. Remember: beware the "get rich quick" methods. It's true that the higher the risk you take, the higher the potential reward. But, more importantly, remember that the chance you take of losing your money is also high.

In your portfolio, if taking the recommended conservative approach, you want to spread more of your money out over money market accounts than stocks. Bonds should take up around half of your investment, as stated before, and your next highest investment should be in the money market. Then you can spread out your remaining investments in stocks. Remember: do not limit yourself to one industry.

There will come a time for rebalancing your investments. Remember: always be active when it comes to your money. Remember: the market is always changing and it is up to you to focus on what is going on and make changes. Say you want to keep half your investment in bonds. Say that your stocks are doing well. Originally you had kept your stock assets at 30%. Now, since your stocks have been doing well, they now make up 40% of your assets. Sell off until you are able to rebalance at 30%.

Also you must be careful with rebalancing. There are taxes and fees. You want to make sure that you are rebalancing at the best time to avoid paying high taxes and fees.

All in all, to grow your wealth it is essential to keep your portfolio diversified. Be patient. Remember that there are always risks. You can decrease these risks by staying active. Know what is going on with your money. Check up on it. Don't take high risks unless you are willing to take high losses. Remember: the conservative route is the safest route. Remember to be patient and stick to your plan. Don't let your emotions get the best of you. Be smart and watch your money.

Before you invest, assess on how much spare cash you have generated every month. Use the bonus free gift "Wealth-Tool" to have a clearer view on your monthly cash flow.

Grab a copy at http://livingthelifeuwant.com/wealth-tool/ if you have not done so. Make use of it, it's free!

Chapter 6
Be Realistic.

Wealth Takes Time.

You are not going to get rich overnight. Let this sink in. You are not going to get rich in a month. Let this sink in. You are not going to get rich in a year. Let this sink in. You are not going to get rich in five years. Let this sink in.

Although this may not be true for everyone, you need to realize that this is the reality of the matter for most. Yes, of course, some get lucky and hit upon an idea, business model, invention, win the lottery, etc. but for the majority, the process of getting rich is years in the making. Decades in the making. Let this sink in. It takes self-discipline, budgeting, adherence to goals, strict money-management, and it takes an income. The more revenue streams the better. It takes smart investing. It takes resilience and perseverance and a never-give-up attitude.

It's going to take belief in your ability to become wealthy. It's going to take someone who is active in every aspect of their money management. It's going to take someone who keeps an eye on their investments. It's going to take someone willing to put their blood, sweat and tears into their financial situation.

Cast aside your fears. Leave your laziness behind. Throw your excuses to the wind. And very importantly, be patient. It's going to take a while and it's going to require that you put your all into becoming wealthy. Those that have made their riches on their own are involved with their equity during every step of its growth. They see their equity as their well-being. It is what they have put so much time, effort and hard work into over years and years. They have waited and they have been patient. And it paid off. And it will pay off for you as long as you are always active and focused. As long as you are willing to stand back up after being knocked down. As long as you learn from being down and out, you will become wealthy. Every misstep is an opportunity to become better. What you have learned here will help you commence your journey towards wealth, but it's up to you to further your financial education.

Look again at the bonus free gift "Wealth-Tool" that you have completed. Be realistic about your goals and savings plan.

Have you downloaded it? Grab a copy at http://livingthelifeuwant.com/wealth-tool/, & you will experience that growing wealth can really be twice as fast.

Conclusion

"Lord, grant that I may always desire more than I can accomplish." – Michelangelo

Never stop striving towards your goals and visions. You don't need to be a famous Renaissance-era artist to live by this statement. But you must always be active and focused toward reaching your goals. Do you still want to live like the wealthy? Do you want to adopt habits that, over the long run, will make you wealthy yourself? Do you want to be rich?

It's up to you to answer these questions. It's up to you to start your journey towards profits and increasing your net worth. You can be given all the advice in the world, read every book on becoming wealthy, and listen to all the rags-to-riches stories you want. In the end, it's always going to be up to you whether you want to become wealthy or not. It's always your choice whether you want to be active in your financial goals or if you want to be passive and just get by. It's up to you if you want laziness and excuses to govern your money. It's also up to you if you decide to take control of your financial destiny and stay active and focused on reaching your goals. It's up to you if you want to believe in yourself. It's up to you to work hard to achieve what you want.

Right now, you can figure out your budget. What's the worst that can happen? You gain a clearer vision of what you can and cannot afford? Maybe you can cut out some extraneous expenses. Maybe you realize what you need to do in order to have extra capital to invest. Maybe by creating a budget for yourself, right now, you can start on the long trek towards wealth.

Right now, you can set goals for yourself. When is the right time? Now is always the right time to begin. The longer you wait—the more you procrastinate—the harder it is going to be to begin. But, remember, it's *always* up to you. You always have the choice to commit yourself toward reaching your goals. You always have the ability to change your ways. People will nudge you to and fro, but you are the one that controls your movements.

Right now, you can begin to manage your money. Every day that you've spent working has been to accrue money. Why not take control over what

27

you've spent your time and hard work to achieve? You can start right at this moment to make the conscious decision to start being the master of your own wealth. You can, at this instant, become a manager of your own money. What's the worst that can happen—you start to build equity? You stop wasting money that can be saved?

Right now, you can pursue extra revenue streams. How about that extra room that's just been housing your extra stuff? Rent it out. How about you put some of that extra stuff you don't need any more up on Ebay? The car you haven't been driving—rent it out. That car you do drive—pick up some passengers through Uber or Lyft to create extra revenue streams.

Right now, you can begin investing in your future. Start watching the stock market. Notice what is going on in the world's financial markets. With the computer and internet, you have every tool you could ever need at your disposal. Figure out where you want to invest. Figure out how you are going to diversify your portfolio. There's never a better time to begin than now.

Take these words as your starting point. There is a long road and hard work ahead. But it will pay off in the long run. Never give up on yourself and your goals and in due time, you will get to where you want to be. Rome wasn't built in a day, but it did get built. Stay active and focused and your vision for the future will become a reality. It may take years. But as long as you adjust your habits and adhere to your goals, you will become wealthy. Be patient.

Words from the Publisher

Thank you so much for purchasing this book and hope you have enjoyed reading and have benefited. If you have enjoyed the book, I would appreciate if you could kindly post a review in Amazon. Even if it is a sentence or two, I would really appreciate it.

For your further reading, please click on the Amazon URL below to see details and for purchase. I really appreciate your continual support.

Thank you very much. God bless!

Books by Lauren Rose

http://www.amazon.com/dp/B013V7ZYHC

http://www.amazon.com/dp/B014AY34H2

http://amazon.com/dp/B014YZOKRU

http://www.amazon.com/dp/B016457AJS